cookies

Cover Slice and bake cookies, page 103.
Photographer Joshua Dasey
Stylist Margot Braddon
Food stylist Nicole Jennings

© ACP Magazines Ltd 2007

This edition first published in 2007 by Metro Books,
by arrangement with ACP Magazines Ltd.
Reprinted 2008.

Metro Books
122 Fifth Avenue
New York, NY 10011

ISBN: 978-1-4351-0016-9

Printed and bound in China by SNP Leefung Printers.

3 5 7 9 10 8 6 4 2

cookies

Pamela Clark

METRO BOOKS
NEW YORK

contents

There's never been a cookie book like this one – full of fantastic and imaginative ideas that will excite the baker as much as the taster. The sensationally original creations you'll find here are so versatile they're the perfect gift for the person who has everything as well as being a child's birthday party-stopper. So, who did steal the cookie from the cookie jar?

malted milk numbers

1 stick butter, softened
½ cup sugar
1 egg
¼ cup honey
¼ cup malted milk powder
2½ cups all-purpose flour
½ teaspoon baking soda
1½ teaspoons cream of tartar
Lemon icing
1 egg white, beaten lightly
1½ cups powdered sugar
2 teaspoons all-purpose flour
2 teaspoons lemon juice,
   approximately
green food coloring

1 Beat butter, sugar and egg in small bowl with electric mixer until combined. Stir in honey and sifted dry ingredients, in two batches.
2 Knead dough on floured surface until smooth; roll dough between sheets of parchment paper until ¼-inch thick. Refrigerate 30 minutes.
3 Preheat oven to 300°F. Grease baking sheets; line with parchment paper.
4 Using 2½-inch number cutters (see page 123), cut 45 numbers from dough; place 1¼ inches apart on baking sheets. Bake about 15 minutes. Cool on baking sheets.
5 Make lemon icing. Spread cookie numbers with icing; set at room temperature.

Lemon icing
Place egg white in small bowl, stir in half the sifted powdered sugar, then remaining sifted powdered sugar, flour and enough lemon juice to make a thick, spreadable icing. Tint icing green.

Makes 45

double chocolate freckles

1 stick butter, softened
¾ cup firmly packed brown sugar
1 egg
1½ cups all-purpose flour
¼ cup self-rising flour
¼ cup cocoa powder
7 ounces dark chocolate, melted
⅓ cup nonpareil sprinkles

1 Beat butter, sugar and egg in small bowl with electric mixer until combined. Stir in sifted dry ingredients, in two batches.
2 Knead dough on floured surface until smooth; roll dough between sheets of parchment paper until ¼-inch thick. Cover; refrigerate 30 minutes.
3 Preheat oven to 350°F. Grease baking sheets; line with parchment paper.
4 Using 1¼-inch, 2-inch and 2½-inch round cutters, cut 14 rounds from dough using each cutter. Place 1¼-inch rounds on one baking sheet; place remainder on other baking sheets.
5 Bake small cookies about 10 minutes; bake larger cookies about 12 minutes. Cool on wire racks.
6 Spread tops of cookies with chocolate; cover with sprinkles. Set at room temperature.

Makes 42

Jumbles are similar to snickerdoodles – but these tasty treats forego the cinnamon-sugar coating, preferring to bake with their spices on the inside.

1 stick butter, softened
½ cup sugar
1 egg
¼ cup honey
2½ cups all-purpose flour
½ teaspoon baking soda
1½ teaspoons cream of tartar
1 teaspoon ground ginger
1 teaspoon ground allspice
½ teaspoon ground cloves

Pink icing
1 egg white, beaten lightly
1½ cups powdered sugar
2 teaspoons all-purpose flour
2 teaspoons lemon juice,
   approximately
pink food coloring

1 Beat butter, sugar and egg in medium bowl with electric mixer until combined. Stir in honey and sifted dry ingredients, in two batches.
2 Knead dough on floured surface until smooth; roll dough between sheets of parchment paper until ¼-inch thick. Cover; refrigerate 30 minutes.
3 Preheat oven to 300°F. Grease baking sheets; line with parchment paper.
4 Using 3½-inch X cutter and 3-inch O cutter (see page 123), cut shapes from dough. Place about 1¼ inches apart on baking sheets.
5 Bake shapes about 15 minutes. Cool on baking sheets.
6 Make pink icing. Spread jumbles with pink icing; set at room temperature.

Pink icing
Place egg white in small bowl, stir in half the sifted powdered sugar; add remaining sifted powdered sugar, flour and enough lemon juice to make a thick spreadable icing. Tint icing pink.

Makes 32

jumble bumbles

choco-cherry macaroon hearts

Try substituting Red Hots in place of the candied cherries for a cinnamon twist on this cookie.

7 tablespoons butter, softened
½ cup sugar
1 egg
2 cups all-purpose flour
1½ tablespoons cocoa powder
3½ ounces dark chocolate, melted

Macaroon filling

1 egg white
¼ cup sugar
½ teaspoon vanilla extract
¾ cup unsweetened shredded coconut
1 teaspoon all-purpose flour
3 tablespoons finely chopped red candied cherries

1 Make macaroon filling.
2 Beat butter, sugar and egg in small bowl with electric mixer until light and fluffy; stir in sifted dry ingredients, in two batches. Stir in chocolate.
3 Knead dough on floured surface until smooth. Roll dough between sheets of parchment paper until ⅓-inch thick.
4 Preheat oven to 350°F. Grease baking sheets; line with parchment paper.
5 Using 3-inch heart-shaped cutter (see page 123), cut hearts from dough. Place, about ¾ inch apart, on baking sheets. Using 1½-inch heart-shaped cutter, cut out centers from hearts.
6 Bake cookies about 7 minutes; remove from oven. Reduce oven temperature to 300°F.
7 Divide macaroon mixture among centers of cookies; smooth surface. Cover with foil (like a tent so foil does not touch surface of macaroon). Bake about 15 minutes or until macaroon is firm. Cool on baking sheets 5 minutes; transfer to wire racks to cool completely.

Macaroon filling

Beat egg white in small bowl with electric mixer until soft peaks form. Gradually add sugar 1 tablespoon at a time, beating until dissolved between additions. Fold in vanilla, coconut, flour and cherries.

Makes 22

choco-cherry bliss bombs

1⅓ cups milk chocolate chips
5 tablespoons butter
¼ cup vegetable oil
⅓ cup sugar
2 eggs
1 cup self-rising flour
1 cup all-purpose flour
6 ounces chocolate-covered
   dried cherries, chopped finely
¼ cup unsweetened shredded
   coconut

1 Stir chocolate, butter, oil and sugar in medium pot over low heat until smooth. Cool 15 minutes.
2 Preheat oven to 350°F. Grease baking sheets; line with parchment paper.
3 Stir eggs and flours into chocolate mixture; stir in cherries.
4 Roll level ½ teaspoons of mixture into balls; roll half the balls in coconut. Place about ¾ inch apart on baking sheets.
5 Bake cookies about 10 minutes. Cool on baking sheets.
6 Serve in paper cones (see page 122).

Makes 280

wedding cake cookies

⅓ cup dried mixed fruit
3 tablespoons brandy
1 stick butter, softened
1 teaspoon finely grated
   orange zest
⅓ cup sugar
1½ tablespoons honey
1 cup self-rising flour
⅔ cup all-purpose flour
½ teaspoon allspice
Fondant icing
10½ ounces white prepared
   fondant, chopped coarsely
1 egg white
½ teaspoon lemon juice
Royal icing
1½ cups pure powdered sugar
1 egg white

1 Process fruit and brandy until smooth.
2 Beat butter, orange zest, sugar and honey in small bowl with electric mixer until combined.
3 Stir in sifted dry ingredients and fruit puree, in two batches.
4 Knead dough on floured surface until smooth; roll dough between sheets of parchment paper until ¼-inch thick. Cover; refrigerate 30 minutes.
5 Preheat oven to 350°F. Grease baking sheets; line with parchment paper.
6 Using 4-inch wedding cake cutter (see page 123), cut 12 shapes from dough. Place about 2 inches apart on baking sheets. Bake about 12 minutes. Cool on wire racks.
7 Make fondant icing. Use a metal spatula, dipped in hot water, to spread icing quickly over cookies; set at room temperature.
8 Make royal icing. Decorate cookies with royal icing.

Fondant icing
Stir fondant in small heatproof bowl over small pot of simmering water until smooth. Add egg white and lemon juice; beat until smooth.

Royal icing
Sift powdered sugar through fine sieve. Beat egg white until foamy in small bowl with electric mixer; beat in powdered sugar, a tablespoon at a time. Cover surface tightly with plastic wrap.

Makes 12

Christmas cake cookies

You can make your own almond meal by grinding blanched almonds in a nut mill or food processor until they reach the consistency of cornmeal.

1⅔ cups all-purpose flour
⅓ cup almond meal
⅓ cup sugar
1 teaspoon allspice
1 teaspoon vanilla extract
1 stick cold butter, chopped
3 tablespoons water
24-ounce rich dark fruit cake
⅓ cup brandy
1 egg white
14 ounces dark chocolate, melted
½ cup white chocolate chips, melted
30 red candied cherries

1 Process flour, almond meal, sugar, allspice, vanilla and butter until crumbly. Add the water, process until ingredients come together.
2 Knead dough on floured surface until smooth; roll dough between sheets of parchment paper until ¼-inch thick. Cover; refrigerate 30 minutes.
3 Preheat oven to 350°F. Grease baking sheets; line with parchment paper.
4 Using 2-inch round cutter (see page 123), cut 30 rounds from dough. Place 1¼ inches apart on baking sheets. Bake 10 minutes.
5 Meanwhile, crumble fruit cake into a medium bowl; add brandy. Press mixture firmly into round metal tablespoon measures. Brush partially baked cookies with egg white, top with cake domes; bake further 5 minutes. Cool on wire racks.
6 Place wire racks over baking sheet; coat cookies with dark chocolate. Set at room temperature.
7 Spoon white chocolate over cookies; top with cherries.

Makes 30

coconut fortune cookies

2 egg whites
⅓ cup sugar
⅓ cup all-purpose flour
1 teaspoon coconut extract
2 tablespoons butter, melted
½ teaspoon finely grated
   lime zest
3 tablespoons unsweetened
   shredded coconut
12 small paper messages

1 Preheat oven to 325°F. Grease baking sheet; line with parchment paper. Draw two 3½-inch circles on paper.
2 Beat egg whites in small bowl with electric mixer until soft peaks form; gradually beat in sugar, beating until dissolved between additions.
3 Fold in sifted flour, coconut extract, butter and lime zest. Drop one rounded tablespoon of mixture into center of each circle on baking sheet, spread evenly to cover circle completely; sprinkle with a little coconut. Bake about 5 minutes.
4 Working quickly, loosen cookies from sheet, place message in the center of cookies; fold in half, then gently bend cookies over edge of a glass (see page 121). Cool for 30 seconds. Transfer to wire rack to cool. Repeat with remaining cookie mixture and coconut.

Makes 12

¼ cup finely chopped
   candied ginger
½ cup finely chopped
   candied pineapple
½ cup finely chopped
   dried papaya
1 cup shredded coconut
1 cup coarsely crushed
   corn flakes
½ cup macadamia nuts,
   chopped finely
¾ cup condensed milk
⅓ cup passion fruit juice or
   pineapple juice
1 cup white chocolate chips

1 Preheat oven to 350°F.
Grease baking sheets; line
with parchment paper.
2 Strain passion fruit pulp; you
need ⅓ cup juice. Discard seeds.
3 Combine ginger, pineapple,
papaya, coconut, corn flakes,
nuts, milk and 3 tablespoons
of the passion fruit juice in
medium bowl.
4 Drop heaping tablespoonfuls
of mixture about 2 inches apart
onto baking sheets; press down
slightly. Bake about 12 minutes.
Cool on baking sheets.
5 Combine chocolate with
remaining passion fruit juice in
small heatproof bowl; stir over
small pot of simmering water
until smooth. Spread chocolate
over flat side of each florentine;
mark with a fork. Set at room
temperature.

Makes 25

tropical florentines

rhubarb custard melting moments

You need to cook 1 large stem chopped rhubarb with about 1½ tablespoons sugar (or to taste) and 1½ tablespoons water over low heat, until rhubarb is pulpy. Drain, cool.

2 sticks butter, softened
½ teaspoon vanilla extract
½ cup powdered sugar
1 cup instant vanilla pudding mix
1 cup all-purpose flour
1½ tablespoons powdered
   sugar, extra

Rhubarb custard

1½ tablespoons instant vanilla
   pudding mix
1½ tablespoons sugar
½ cup milk
⅓ cup stewed rhubarb

1 Preheat oven to 325°F. Grease baking sheets; line with parchment paper.
2 Make rhubarb custard.
3 Beat butter, vanilla and sifted powdered sugar in small bowl with electric mixer until light and fluffy.
4 Stir in sifted pudding mix and flour in two batches.
5 With floured hands, roll rounded teaspoons of mixture into balls. Place about 2 inches apart on baking sheets; flatten slightly with a floured fork.
6 Bake about 15 minutes. Let stand 5 minutes; cool on wire racks.
7 Sandwich cookies with a little rhubarb custard.

Rhubarb custard

Blend pudding mix and sugar with milk in small pot; stir over medium heat until mixture boils and thickens. Remove from heat, stir in rhubarb. Cover surface of custard with plastic wrap; refrigerate until cold.

Makes 25

hot cross bun cookies

You can make your own almond meal by grinding blanched almonds in a nut mill or food processor until they reach the consistency of cornmeal.

1 stick butter, softened
⅔ cup sugar
1 egg
¼ cup finely chopped mixed
   candied fruit peel
½ cup dried currants
2 cups self-rising flour
1 teaspoon allspice
2 teaspoons milk
3 tablespoons almond meal
3½ ounces marzipan
3 tablespoons apricot jam,
   warmed, strained

1 Preheat oven to 325°F. Grease baking sheets, line with parchment paper.
2 Beat butter, sugar and egg in small bowl with electric mixer until light and fluffy. Stir in candied peel, currants, sifted flour and spice, and milk in two batches.
3 Roll rounded teaspoons of mixture into balls; place about 2 inches apart on baking sheets.
4 Knead almond meal into marzipan. Roll marzipan into ¼-inch diameter sausages; cut into 1½-inch lengths.
5 Brush cookies with a little milk; place marzipan crosses on cookies, press down gently.
6 Bake about 15 minutes. Brush cookies with jam; Cool on baking sheets.

Makes 48

date and walnut scrolls

1 stick butter, softened
⅓ cup sugar
1 teaspoon ground cardamom
1 egg
1½ cups all-purpose flour
1 cup walnuts, roasted,
   ground finely
2 cups dried dates,
   chopped coarsely
¼ cup sugar, extra
2 teaspoons finely grated
   lemon zest
⅓ cup lemon juice
¼ teaspoon ground cardamom,
   extra
½ cup water

1 Beat butter, sugar, cardamom and egg in small bowl with electric mixer until combined. Stir in sifted flour and walnuts.
2 Knead dough on floured surface until smooth; divide into two portions. Roll each portion between sheets of parchment paper to 6- x 12-inch rectangles; refrigerate 20 minutes.
3 Meanwhile, stir dates, extra sugar, lemon zest and juice, extra cardamom and the water in medium pot over medium heat, without boiling, until sugar is dissolved; bring to a boil. Reduce heat, simmer, uncovered, stirring occasionally, 5 minutes or until mixture is thick and pulpy. Transfer to large bowl; refrigerate 10 minutes.

4 Spread filling evenly over the two rectangles, leaving ½-inch border. Using paper as a guide, roll rectangles tightly from short side to enclose filling. Wrap rolls in parchment paper; refrigerate 30 minutes.
5 Preheat oven to 375°F. Grease baking sheets; line with parchment paper.
6 Trim edges of roll; cut each roll into ½-inch slices. Place slices cut-side up on baking sheets; bake about 20 minutes.

Makes 28

almond and plum crescents

You can make your own almond meal by grinding blanched almonds in a nut mill or food processor until they reach the consistency of cornmeal.

1½ cups all-purpose flour
½ cup almond meal
¼ cup sugar
2 teaspoons finely grated
    lemon zest
3 ounces cream cheese,
    chopped
5½ tablespoons butter,
    chopped
3 tablespoons buttermilk
1 egg white
¼ cup sliced almonds,
    crushed lightly
Filling
⅓ cup finely chopped
    pitted prunes
¼ cup plum jam
¼ cup sugar
½ teaspoon ground cinnamon

1 Process flour, almond meal, sugar and lemon zest until combined. Add cream cheese and butter, pulse until crumbly. Add buttermilk, process until ingredients come together.
2 Knead dough on floured surface until smooth. Divide dough in half. Roll each half between sheets of parchment paper until large enough to be cut into 9-inch rounds; cut dough using 9-inch cake pan as a guide. Discard excess dough. Cover rounds; refrigerate 30 minutes.
3 Preheat oven to 350°F. Grease baking sheets; line with parchment paper.
4 Make filling by combining ingredients in small bowl.
5 Cut each round into eight wedges, spread each wedge with a little filling mixture; roll from the wide end into a crescent shape. Place on baking sheets, brush with egg white, sprinkle with sliced almonds. Bake about 25 minutes. Cool on baking sheets.

Makes 16

apple crumble custard creams

1 medium fresh apple, peeled, cored, chopped coarsely
2 teaspoons water
1 stick butter, softened
⅓ cup firmly packed brown sugar
3 tablespoons apple juice concentrate
1 cup self-rising flour
¾ cup all-purpose flour
¼ cup oat bran
¼ cup unsweetened shredded coconut
1 teaspoon ground cinnamon
1½ tablespoons powdered sugar

Custard cream
1½ tablespoons instant vanilla pudding mix
1½ tablespoons sugar
½ cup milk
¼ teaspoon vanilla extract
4 ounces cream cheese, softened

1 Stew apple with the water in small pot, covered, over medium heat until tender. Mash with a fork; cool.
2 Beat butter, sugar and apple concentrate in small bowl with electric mixer until combined.
3 Stir in sifted flours, oat-bran, stewed apple, coconut and cinnamon, in two batches.
4 Knead dough on floured surface until smooth. Roll dough between sheets of parchment paper until ⅛-inch thick; refrigerate 30 minutes.
5 Preheat oven to 350°F. Grease baking sheets; line with parchment paper.
6 Using 2½-inch apple cutter (see page 123), cut 40 shapes from dough. Place shapes about 1¼ inches apart on baking sheets. Bake about 12 minutes. Cool on wire racks.
7 Meanwhile, make custard cream.
8 Sandwich cookies with custard cream. Serve dusted with sifted powdered sugar.

Custard cream
Blend pudding mix and sugar with milk and vanilla in small pot; stir over medium heat until mixture boils and thickens. Remove from heat, cover surface with plastic wrap; cool. Beat cream cheese in small bowl with electric mixer until smooth. Add custard; beat until combined.

Makes 20

1 stick butter, softened
2 teaspoons finely grated
   lemon zest
½ teaspoon almond extract
½ cup sugar
1 egg
1⅔ cups all-purpose flour
1 egg white
nonpareils or other rainbow
   sprinkles
12 popsicle sticks
6 ounces individually wrapped
   sugar-free lollipops

1 Beat butter, lemon zest, almond extract, sugar and egg in small bowl with electric mixer until combined. Stir in sifted flour, in two batches.
2 Knead dough on floured surface until smooth; roll dough between sheets of parchment paper until ¼-inch thick. Cover; refrigerate 30 minutes.
3 Meanwhile, using rolling pin, gently tap wrapped lollipops to crush slightly. Unwrap lollipops; separate by color into small bowls.
4 Preheat oven to 350°F. Grease baking sheets; line with parchment paper.
5 Using 4-inch round cutter (see page 123), cut 12 rounds from dough. Place 2 inches apart on baking sheets.

6 Place 1-inch, 2-inch and 3-inch cutters starting from the center of each 4-inch round. Remove dough between 2-inch and 3-inch cutters; remove dough from center of 1-inch cutter (see page 121). Brush half the remaining dough with egg white, sprinkle with sprinkles. Slide one popsicle stick under each cookie (see page 121).
7 Bake about 10 minutes. Remove baking sheets from oven, fill gaps with crushed lollipops; bake further 5 minutes. Cool on sheets.

Makes 12

stained-glass lollipops

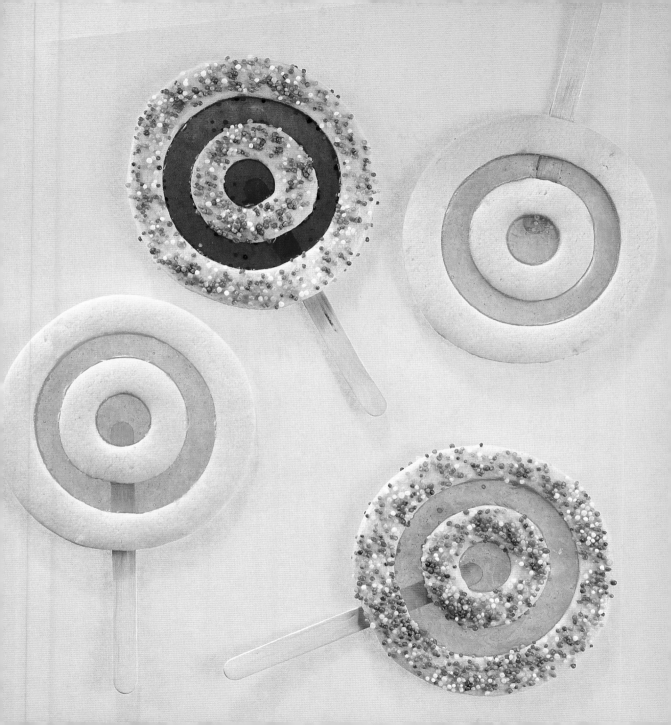

dancing shoes

1 stick butter, softened
¾ cup firmly packed
   brown sugar
1 egg
1½ cups all-purpose flour
¼ cup self-rising flour
¼ cup cocoa powder
3½ ounces dark chocolate,
   melted
silver nonpareils

Colored sugar

⅔ cup sugar
pink, yellow, green and purple
   food coloring

1 Beat butter, sugar and egg in small bowl with electric mixer until combined. Stir in sifted flours and cocoa in two batches.
2 Knead dough on floured surface until smooth; roll dough between sheets of parchment paper until ¼-inch thick. Cover; refrigerate 30 minutes.
3 Preheat oven to 350°F. Grease baking sheets; line with parchment paper.
4 Using a 3-inch shoe-shaped cutter, cut 25 shapes from dough. Place about 1¼ inches apart on sheets. Bake about 12 minutes. Cool on baking sheets.
5 Make colored sugar.
6 Spread cookies with chocolate. Sprinkle shoes with colored sugar; decorate with nonpareils.

Colored sugar
Divide sugar among four small plastic bags. Add different coloring to each bag to tint sugar. Rub coloring into sugar until combined.

Makes 25

ice-cream cones

2 egg whites
⅓ cup sugar
⅓ cup all-purpose flour
2 tablespoons butter, melted
½ teaspoon vanilla extract
2 teaspoons cocoa powder
ice-cream

1 Preheat oven to 350°F. Grease baking sheet; line with parchment paper. Mark a 4-inch circle on paper.

2 Beat egg whites in small bowl with electric mixer until soft peaks form; gradually beat in sugar, beating until dissolved between additions. Stir in sifted flour, butter and vanilla.

3 Place ¼ cup of the mixture in small bowl, stir in sifted cocoa; spoon into a piping bag fitted with a small plain tube.

4 Place a rounded tablespoon of remaining mixture in center of each circle on sheet, spread evenly to fill circles. Pipe chocolate stripes across circles (see page 119).

5 Bake about 5 minutes. Working quickly, lift cookies from sheet, shape into cones (see page 119). Cool on wire racks. Repeat with remaining cookie mixture.

6 Just before serving, fill cookie cones with ice-cream.

Makes 10

1 stick butter, softened
2 teaspoons finely grated
   orange zest
1 cup firmly packed brown sugar
1⅓ cups whole-wheat flour
1½ teaspoons baking powder
½ teaspoon salt
1 cup walnuts, roasted,
   chopped coarsely
⅔ cup raisins, halved
2 teaspoons dried rosemary
⅓ cup orange juice
⅔ cup unsweetened shredded
   coconut
⅔ cup rolled oats

1 Preheat oven to 350°F. Grease baking sheets; line with parchment paper.
2 Beat butter, zest and sugar in small bowl with electric mixer until combined. Transfer to medium bowl; stir in flour, baking powder and salt; then stir in remaining ingredients.
3 Roll rounded tablespoons of mixture into balls, place about 2 inches apart on baking sheets; flatten slightly. Bake 15 minutes. Cool on baking sheets.

Makes 28

whole-wheat rosemary butter rounds

decadent mocha fingers

1 teaspoon instant coffee
  granules
2 teaspoons boiling water
1 stick butter, softened
¾ cup firmly packed
  brown sugar
1 egg
1½ cups all-purpose flour
¼ cup self-rising flour
¼ cup cocoa powder
75 roasted coffee beans

Mocha custard
3 tablespoons instant vanilla
  pudding mix
3 tablespoons sugar
2 ounces dark chocolate,
  chopped roughly
1 cup milk
1½ tablespoons coffee liqueur

1 Blend coffee with the water. Beat butter, sugar and egg in small bowl with electric mixer until combined. Stir in coffee mixture, sifted flours and cocoa, in two batches.
2 Knead dough on floured surface until smooth; roll dough between sheets of parchment paper until ¼-inch thick. Cover; refrigerate 30 minutes.
3 Preheat oven to 350°F. Grease baking sheets; line with parchment paper.
4 Make mocha custard.
5 Using 3-inch square cutter (see page 123), cut out 25 shapes from dough. Halve squares to make 50 rectangles; place on baking sheets. Press three coffee beans on half of the rectangles.
6 Bake about 12 minutes. Cool on wire racks.
7 Spread mocha custard over plain cookies; top with coffee-bean topped cookies.

Mocha custard
Blend pudding mix, sugar and chocolate with milk in small pot; stir over medium heat until mixture boils and thickens. Remove from heat, stir in liqueur. Cover surface with plastic wrap; refrigerate until cold.

Makes 25

double choc-n-chili cookies

2 sticks butter, softened
1 teaspoon vanilla extract
¾ cup sugar
¾ cup firmly packed brown
   sugar
1 egg
2 cups all-purpose flour
¼ cup cocoa powder
1 teaspoon baking soda
14 ounces dark chocolate,
   chopped coarsely

Candied chilies

¼ cup sugar
¼ cup water
3 fresh red Thai chilies,
   chopped finely

1 Preheat oven to 350°F. Grease baking sheets; line with parchment paper.
2 Make candied chilies.
3 Beat butter, vanilla, sugars and egg in small bowl with electric mixer until light and fluffy; transfer to large bowl.
4 Stir in sifted flour, cocoa and baking soda in two batches. Stir in candied chilies and chocolate.
5 Roll level tablespoons of dough into balls; place about 2 inches apart on baking sheets. Bake about 12 minutes. Cool on baking sheets.

Candied chilies

Stir sugar and the water in small pot over medium heat until sugar dissolves. Add chilies, boil, 2 minutes; cool. Strain, discard syrup.

Makes 48

jammy flowers

You can make your own almond meal by grinding blanched almonds in a nut mill or food processor until they reach the consistency of cornmeal.

1 stick butter, softened
½ teaspoon vanilla extract
½ cup sugar
1 cup almond meal
1 egg
1 cup all-purpose flour
1 teaspoon finely grated
   lemon zest
⅓ cup raspberry jam
3 tablespoons apricot jam

1 Preheat oven to 350°F. Grease baking sheets; line with parchment paper.
2 Beat butter, vanilla, sugar and almond meal in small bowl with electric mixer until light and fluffy. Add egg, beat until combined; stir in sifted flour.
3 Divide lemon zest between both jams; mix well.
4 Roll rounded tablespoons of mixture into balls; place about 2 inches apart on baking sheets, flatten slightly. Using end of a wooden spoon, press a flower shape (about ½-inch deep) into dough; fill each hole with a little jam, using apricot jam for centers of flowers.
5 Bake about 15 minutes. Cool on baking sheets.

Makes 26

2 sticks butter, softened
1 teaspoon vanilla extract
¾ cup sugar
¾ cup firmly packed
   brown sugar
1 egg
2 cups all-purpose flour
¼ cup cocoa powder
1 teaspoon baking soda
⅓ cup finely chopped
   roasted hazelnuts
⅔ cup coarsely chopped
   dark chocolate
⅔ cup coarsely chopped
   milk chocolate
⅔ cup coarsely chopped
   white chocolate

1 Preheat oven to 350°F.
Grease baking sheets; line
with parchment paper.
2 Beat butter, vanilla, sugars and
egg in small bowl with electric
mixer until light and fluffy;
transfer to large bowl.
3 Stir in sifted flour, cocoa and
baking soda in two batches.
Stir in nuts and chocolate.
4 Roll rounded tablespoons of
dough into balls; place about
2 inches apart on baking sheets.
Bake about 12 minutes. Cool on
baking sheets.

Makes 48

chocolate fudge brownies

macadamia anzacs

Anzac cookies are an Australian special – named in honor of the Australian and New Zealand Army Corps, preferred by soldiers and schoolchildren alike. The recipe is thought to be descended from Scottish oatmeal cookies. Wherever it came from, it's considered delicious the world over.

1 stick butter, chopped
3 tablespoons honey
½ teaspoon baking soda
3 tablespoons boiling water
1 cup rolled oats
1 cup all-purpose flour
1 cup firmly packed brown sugar
¾ cup unsweetened shredded
   coconut
½ cup finely chopped
   macadamia nuts
¼ cup finely chopped
   candied ginger

1 Preheat oven to 350°F. Grease baking sheets; line with parchment paper.
2 Combine butter and honey in medium pot, stir over low heat until smooth.
3 Stir in combined baking soda and the water; stir in remaining ingredients.
4 Roll rounded tablespoons of mixture into balls. Place about 2 inches apart on baking sheets; flatten slightly. Bake 15 minutes. Cool on baking sheets.

Makes 32

jigsaw gingerbread people

1 stick butter, softened
½ cup firmly packed
   brown sugar
1 egg yolk
2½ cups all-purpose flour
1 teaspoon baking soda
3 teaspoons ground ginger
½ cup honey
Lemon icing
1 egg white, beaten lightly
1½ cups powdered sugar
2 teaspoons all-purpose flour
2 teaspoons lemon juice,
   approximately
yellow food coloring

1 Preheat oven to 350°F. Grease baking sheets; line with parchment paper.
2 Beat butter, sugar and egg yolk in small bowl with electric mixer until smooth; transfer to large bowl. Stir in sifted dry ingredients and honey in two batches.
3 Knead dough on floured surface until smooth.
4 Divide dough in half; roll each half between sheets of parchment paper until ¼-inch thick.
5 Place dough on baking sheet. Using gingerbread people template, cut around shapes; remove excess dough (see pages 116 & 119). Roll excess dough between sheets of parchment paper until ¼-inch thick. Place dough on baking sheet. Using heart template, cut around shape; remove excess dough (see pages 116 & 119). Bake shapes about 15 minutes. Cool on baking sheets.
6 Make lemon icing. Spread cookies with icing; set at room temperature.

Lemon icing
Place egg white in small bowl, stir in half the sifted powdered sugar; stir in remaining sifted powdered sugar, flour and enough juice to make a spreadable icing. Tint icing until lemon-colored.

Makes 24 pieces

mud cake sandwiches

2 sticks butter, softened
1½ cups firmly packed
   brown sugar
2 eggs
3 cups all-purpose flour
½ cup self-rising flour
½ cup cocoa powder
3 tablespoons cocoa powder,
   extra

Chocolate mud cake

1 stick plus 2 tablespoons
   butter, chopped
3½ ounces dark chocolate,
   chopped coarsely
1 cup sugar
½ cup water
3 tablespoons coffee liqueur
1 cup all-purpose flour
3 tablespoons cocoa powder
2 egg yolks

Chocolate ganache

⅓ cup heavy cream
7 ounces dark chocolate,
   chopped coarsely

1 Preheat oven to 325°F. Grease two 8- x 12-inch shallow baking pans; line with a strip of parchment paper, extending paper ¾ inches above edges of pans.
2 Make chocolate mud cake.
3 Make chocolate ganache.
4 Beat butter, sugar and eggs in small bowl with electric mixer until combined. Transfer mixture to large bowl; stir in sifted flours and cocoa, in two batches. Knead dough on floured surface until smooth; divide in half, roll each portion between sheets of parchment paper until ¼-inch thick. Refrigerate 30 minutes.
5 Preheat oven to 350°F. Grease baking sheets; line with parchment paper.
6 Using 2½-inch round cutter (see page 123), cut 48 rounds from dough. Place 1¼ inches apart on baking sheets. Bake 12 minutes. Cool on wire racks.
7 Spread ganache onto underside of cookies; sandwich a mud cake round between two cookies.
8 Using heart template (see page 116), dust cookies with extra cocoa.

Chocolate mud cake
Combine butter, chocolate, sugar, the water and liqueur in small pot. Stir over low heat until smooth. Place mixture in medium bowl; cool 10 minutes. Whisk in sifted flour and cocoa, then egg yolks. Divide mixture among pans. Bake 25 minutes. Cool cakes in pans. Using 2½-inch round cutter (see page 123), cut 12 rounds from each cake.

Chocolate ganache
Bring cream to a boil in small pot; remove from heat. Add chocolate; stir until smooth. Refrigerate until spreadable.

Makes 24

choco-nut mint stacks

You will need about a pound of chocolate after-dinner mints for this recipe.

1 stick butter, softened
¾ cup firmly packed
   brown sugar
1 egg
1½ cups all-purpose flour
¼ cup self-rising flour
3 tablespoons unsweetened
   shredded coconut
½ teaspoon coconut extract
3 tablespoons cocoa powder
40 square after-dinner mints

1 Beat butter, sugar and egg in small bowl with electric mixer until combined. Stir in sifted flours in two batches. Place half the mixture into another small bowl; stir in coconut and extract. Stir sifted cocoa into the other bowl.
2 Knead each portion of dough on floured surface until smooth. Roll between sheets of parchment paper until ⅛-inch thick. Cover; refrigerate 30 minutes.
3 Preheat oven to 350°F. Grease baking sheets; line with parchment paper.
4 Using 2½-inch square cutter (see page 123), cut 30 shapes from each portion of dough. Place about 1¼ inches apart on baking sheets.
5 Bake about 8 minutes. While cookies are still hot, sandwich three warm alternate-flavored cookies with after-dinner mints; press down gently. Cool on baking sheets.

Makes 20

chocolate-kissed dominoes

5½ tablespoons butter,
   softened
½ cup firmly packed
   brown sugar
1 egg
¼ cup unsweetened
   shredded coconut
¼ cup wheat germ
¾ cup whole-wheat
   all-purpose flour
⅓ cup white self-rising flour
¼ cup dark chocolate mini
   chips, approximately
5 ounces dark chocolate, melted

1 Beat butter and sugar in small bowl with electric mixer until smooth; add egg, beat until combined. Stir in coconut, wheat germ and sifted flours.

2 Roll dough between sheets of parchment paper until ¼-inch thick. Cover; refrigerate 30 minutes.

3 Preheat oven to 350°F. Grease baking sheets; line with parchment paper.

4 Using 3½-inch square cutter (see page 123), cut 14 squares from dough; cut each square in half to make 28 rectangles. Place about 1¼ inches apart on baking sheets. Using a knife, mark (do not cut through) each rectangle across the center, to make two squares. Press chocolate bits into each square to make dominoes.

5 Bake about 12 minutes. Cool on baking sheets.

6 Spread bases of dominoes with melted chocolate; set at room temperature on parchment-paper-lined baking sheets.

Makes 28

lemon-glazed Christmas wreaths

3 cups self-rising flour
1 stick butter, chopped
¼ cup milk
⅔ cup sugar
1 teaspoon vanilla extract
2 eggs
edible silver glitter, to decorate
Lemon icing
3 cups powdered sugar
3 tablespoons lemon juice,
    approximately

1 Preheat oven to 350°F. Grease baking sheets; line with parchment paper.
2 Sift flour into medium bowl, rub in butter. Combine milk and sugar in small pot, stir over low heat until sugar is dissolved, add vanilla; cool 5 minutes. Stir combined warm milk mixture and egg into flour mixture.
3 Knead dough on floured surface until smooth.
4 Roll rounded teaspoons of dough into 5-inch sausages. Twist two sausages together, form into circles; press edges together. Place about 1¼ inches apart on baking sheets.
5 Bake about 15 minutes. Cool on wire racks.
6 Meanwhile, make lemon icing. Drizzle wreaths with icing; set at room temperature. Sprinkle with edible glitter.

Lemon icing
Sift powdered sugar into small heatproof bowl; stir in enough juice to make a firm paste. Stir over small pot of simmering water until pourable.

Makes 30

lemongrass, ginger and sesame bars

You will need eight 1-ounce packages of original sesame candy for this recipe; look for this treat in gourmet grocers, health-food stores, or specialty stores that carry international sweets. Lemongrass can be purchased at gourmet grocery stores or Asian markets; be sure to buy it fresh, not frozen or dried.

1 stick butter, softened
⅔ cup firmly packed
   brown sugar
½ teaspoon ground cardamom
½ teaspoon ground cinnamon
pinch ground nutmeg
pinch ground clove
2 egg yolks
1½ cups all-purpose flour
4-inch stick fresh lemongrass,
   chopped finely
3 tablespoons finely chopped
   candied ginger
32 sesame candies

1 Beat butter, sugar, spices and egg yolks in small bowl with electric mixer until smooth. Stir in sifted flour, lemongrass and ginger.
2 Knead dough on floured surface until smooth. Roll dough between sheets of parchment paper until ¼-inch thick; refrigerate 30 minutes.
3 Preheat oven to 325°F. Grease baking sheets; line with parchment paper.
4 Using 3½-inch square cutter (see page 123), cut 16 shapes from dough; cut in half to make 32 rectangles. Place 2 inches apart on baking sheets. Bake 12 minutes.
5 Carefully trim edges of sesame candy to fit the top of each cookie. Top each hot cookie with a sesame candy; bake 3 minutes. Cool on baking sheets.

Makes 32

peanut brittle cookies

1 stick butter, softened
¼ cup crunchy peanut butter
½ cup firmly packed
   brown sugar
1 egg
1½ cups all-purpose flour
½ teaspoon baking soda
Peanut brittle
¾ cup roasted unsalted peanuts
½ cup sugar
3 tablespoons water

1 Preheat oven to 325°F.
Grease baking sheets; line
with parchment paper.
2 Make peanut brittle.
3 Beat butter, peanut butter,
sugar and egg in small bowl with
electric mixer until combined.
Stir in sifted dry ingredients and
crushed peanut brittle.
4 Roll heaped teaspoons of
mixture into balls with floured
hands. Place about 2 inches
apart on baking sheets; flatten
slightly with hand.
5 Bake about 12 minutes. Cool
on baking sheets.

Peanut brittle
Place nuts on parchment-paper-
lined baking sheet. Combine
sugar and the water in small
skillet, stir over medium heat,
without boiling, until sugar is
dissolved. Bring to a boil; boil,
uncovered, without stirring, until
golden brown. Pour mixture
over nuts; leave until set. Crush
coarsely in food processor.

Makes 42

chocolate-orange jelly cakes

½ cup sugar

2 eggs

1 cup all-purpose flour

3 tablespoons sugar, extra

14 ounces dark chocolate, melted

3 slices candied orange, cut into wedges

Orange jelly

1 cup orange juice

3 tablespoons orange marmalade

3-ounce package orange gelatin mix

1 Make orange jelly.

2 Preheat oven to 350°F. Grease baking sheets; line with parchment paper.

3 Spread sugar evenly over base of shallow baking sheet; heat in oven until sugar feels hot to touch. Beat eggs in small bowl with electric mixer on high speed for 1 minute; add hot sugar, beat about 10 minutes or until mixture is thick and will hold its shape.

4 Meanwhile, sift flour three times. Fit large piping bag with plain ½-inch tube.

5 Transfer egg mixture to large bowl, fold in sifted flour. Place mixture into piping bag. Pipe 1½-inch rounds of mixture onto baking sheets, 1¼ inches apart.

6 Sprinkle each round evenly with extra sugar. Bake each sheet, one at a time, about 4 minutes. Cool on baking sheets.

7 Lift jelly from pan to cutting board. Using a 1½-inch round cutter (see page 123), cut out 25 shapes.

8 Top each sponge cake with a round of jelly, place on wire rack over baking sheet; coat with chocolate. When chocolate is almost set, top with candied orange wedges.

Orange jelly

Combine juice and marmalade in small pot, bring to a boil; remove from heat. Add gelatin crystals, stir until dissolved; cool. Line a deep 9-inch-square cake pan with parchment paper, extending paper 2 inches above edges of pan. Pour jelly into pan; refrigerate until set.

Makes 25

chocolate ginger Easter eggs

1 stick butter, softened
¾ cup firmly packed
  brown sugar
1 egg
3 tablespoons finely chopped
  candied ginger
1½ cups all-purpose flour
¼ cup self-rising flour
¼ cup cocoa powder

Chocolate fondant icing
10½ ounces chocolate prepared
  fondant, chopped coarsely
1 egg white, beaten lightly

Royal icing
1½ cups pure powdered sugar
1 egg white
pink, green, blue and yellow
  food coloring

1 Beat butter, sugar and egg in small bowl with electric mixer until combined. Stir in ginger then sifted flours and cocoa, in two batches.
2 Knead dough on floured surface until smooth. Roll dough between sheets of parchment paper until ¼-inch thick; refrigerate 30 minutes.
3 Preheat oven to 350°F. Grease baking sheets; line with parchment paper.
4 Using 1-inch, 1½-inch, 2-inch and 3-inch oval cutters (see page 123), cut 13 shapes from dough with each cutter. Place 1¼ inches apart on baking sheets.
5 Bake small cookies about 10 minutes; bake larger cookies about 12 minutes. Cool on wire racks.
6 Make chocolate fondant icing. Use a metal spatula, dipped in hot water, to spread icing quickly over cookies. Set at room temperature.
7 Make royal icing. Divide icing among four bowls. Tint each bowl with food coloring; use to pipe patterns on cookies.

Chocolate fondant icing
Stir fondant in small heatproof bowl over small pot of simmering water until smooth. Stir in egg white. Let stand at room temperature about 10 minutes or until thickened slightly.

Royal icing
Sift powdered sugar through fine sieve. Beat egg white until foamy in small bowl with electric mixer; beat in powdered sugar, one tablespoon at a time. Cover surface tightly with plastic wrap.

Makes 52

honey, oat and barley horseshoes

1 stick butter, softened
½ cup sugar
1 egg
3 tablespoons honey
3 tablespoons maple syrup
½ cup rolled oats
½ cup rolled barley
2 cups all-purpose flour
½ teaspoon baking soda
1½ teaspoons cream of tartar
1 teaspoon ground ginger
1 teaspoon allspice
½ teaspoon ground cloves
½ cup rolled oats, extra

1 Preheat oven to 350°F. Grease baking sheets; line with parchment paper.
2 Beat butter, sugar and egg in small bowl with electric mixer until combined. Transfer to large bowl; stir in honey, maple syrup, oats, barley and sifted dry ingredients.
3 Knead dough on floured surface until smooth. Sprinkle surface with extra rolled oats; roll level tablespoons of dough in oats into 5-inch sausages.
4 Shape into horseshoes; place about 1¼ inches apart on baking sheets. Bake about 20 minutes. Cool on wire racks.

Makes 26

2 instant latte packets
(about 1 ounce mix total)
1½ tablespoons boiling water
1 stick butter, softened
¾ cup firmly packed brown
sugar
1 egg
1½ cups all-purpose flour
¼ cup self-rising flour

1 Blend contents of latte packets with the water in small bowl.
2 Beat butter, sugar, egg and latte paste in small bowl with electric mixer until combined. Stir in sifted flours in two batches.
3 Knead dough on floured surface until smooth; roll dough between sheets of parchment paper until ¼-inch thick. Cover; refrigerate 30 minutes.
4 Preheat oven to 350°F. Grease baking sheets; line with parchment paper.
5 Using a fancy 3-inch square cutter (see page 123), cut out 30 squares. Place squares on baking sheets. Stamp center of each cookie with a floured rubber stamp (see pages 116 & 118).
6 Bake about 15 minutes. Cool on wire racks.

Makes 30

girl-about-town latte squares

pink macaroons

You can make your own almond meal by grinding blanched almonds in a nut mill or food processor until they reach the consistency of cornmeal.

3 egg whites
3 tablespoons sugar
pink food coloring
1¼ cups powdered sugar
1 cup almond meal
3 tablespoons powdered sugar, extra

White chocolate ganache
3½ ounces white chocolate, chopped coarsely
3 tablespoons heavy cream

1 Make white chocolate ganache.
2 Grease baking sheets; line with parchment paper.
3 Beat egg whites in small bowl with electric mixer until soft peaks form. Add sugar and food coloring, beat until sugar dissolves. Transfer mixture to large bowl. Fold in sifted powdered sugar and almond meal, in two batches.
4 Spoon mixture into large piping bag fitted with ½-inch plain tube. Pipe thirty-six 1½-inch rounds, ¾-inch apart, onto baking sheets. Tap sheets on counter top to allow macaroons to spread slightly. Dust with sifted extra powdered sugar; let stand 15 minutes.
5 Preheat oven to 300°F.
6 Bake macaroons 20 minutes. Let stand 5 minutes; transfer to wire rack to cool.
7 Sandwich macaroons with ganache. Dust with a little sifted powdered sugar, if desired.

White chocolate ganache
Stir chocolate and cream in small pot over low heat until smooth. Transfer mixture to small bowl. Cover; refrigerate until mixture is spreadable.

Makes 18

shortbread buttons

2 sticks butter, softened
⅓ cup sugar
¼ cup rice flour
2¼ cups all-purpose flour
1½ tablespoons sugar, extra

1 Preheat oven to 300°F. Grease baking sheets; line with parchment paper.
2 Beat butter and sugar in small bowl with electric mixer until smooth. Stir in sifted flours. Knead dough on floured surface until smooth.
3 Place 2-inch round floured cutter (see page 123) on an baking sheet, press one level tablespoon of dough evenly inside the cutter, remove cutter (see page 118). Repeat with remaining dough.
4 Use the lid of a plastic water bottle to indent the buttons. Use a skewer to make holes in buttons. Use a fork to make pattern around edges of buttons (see page 118).
5 Sprinkle buttons with extra sugar. Bake 30 minutes or until firm. Cool on baking sheets.

Makes 26

caramel ginger crunchies

2 cups all-purpose flour
½ teaspoon baking soda
1 teaspoon ground cinnamon
2 teaspoons ground ginger
1 cup sugar
1 stick cold butter, chopped
1 egg
1 teaspoon honey
3 tablespoons finely chopped
   candied ginger
45 wrapped hard caramels

1 Preheat oven to 325°F.
Grease baking sheets; line
with parchment paper.
2 Process sifted dry ingredients
with butter until mixture is
crumbly; add egg, honey and
ginger, process until ingredients
come together. Knead on
floured surface until smooth.
3 Roll rounded teaspoons of
mixture into balls; flatten slightly.
Place about 1¼ inches apart on
baking sheets.
4 Bake 13 minutes. Place one
caramel on top of each hot
cookie. Bake about 7 minutes
or until caramel begins to melt.
Cool on baking sheets.

Makes 45

Christmas angels

1 stick butter, softened
¾ cup sugar
1 egg
1½ cups all-purpose flour
¼ cup self-rising flour
½ cup unsweetened shredded
    coconut
⅓ cup apricot jam, warmed,
    strained

Macaroon topping

3 egg whites
¾ cup sugar
¼ cup all-purpose flour
2¼ cups unsweetened shredded
    coconut

1 Beat butter, sugar and egg in small bowl with electric mixer until light and fluffy. Stir in sifted flours and coconut in two batches.
2 Knead dough on floured surface until smooth; roll dough between sheets of parchment paper until ¼-inch thick. Cover; refrigerate 30 minutes.
3 Preheat oven to 350°F. Grease baking sheets; line with parchment paper.
4 Make macaroon topping.
5 Using 4½-inch angel cutter (see page 123), cut 16 angel shapes from dough. Place, about 1¼ inches apart, on baking sheets.
6 Bake 8 minutes. Spread each hot cookie with jam; divide macaroon topping among angels. Cover with foil (like a tent so foil does not touch surface of macaroon). Bake 7 minutes. Cool on wire racks.

Macaroon topping
Beat egg whites in small bowl with electric mixer until soft peaks form. Gradually add sugar, beating until dissolved between additions. Fold in sifted flour and coconut in two batches.

Makes 16

green tea and almond tiles

You can make your own almond meal by grinding blanched almonds in a nut mill or food processor until they reach the consistency of cornmeal.

1 stick butter, softened
¼ cup sugar
½ teaspoon vanilla extract
1 egg
1 cup all-purpose flour
3 tablespoons self-rising flour
¼ cup cornstarch
1½ tablespoons green tea leaves (about 4 tea bags)
½ cup almond meal
Fondant icing
10½ ounces white prepared fondant, chopped coarsely
1 egg white, beaten lightly
Royal icing
1½ cups pure powdered sugar
1 egg white
½ teaspoon vanilla extract
black food coloring

1 Beat butter, sugar, vanilla and egg in small bowl with electric mixer until light and fluffy. Stir in sifted flours, tea and almond meal.
2 Knead dough on floured surface until smooth; roll dough between sheets of parchment paper until ¼-inch thick. Cover, refrigerate 30 minutes.
3 Preheat oven to 350°F. Grease baking sheets; line with parchment paper.
4 Using 4-inch square cutter (see page 123), cut 14 squares from dough. Cut squares in half to make 28 rectangles. Place about 1¼ inches apart on baking sheets.
5 Bake about 15 minutes. Cool on wire racks.
6 Make fondant icing. Make royal icing.
7 Using a metal spatula dipped in hot water, spread cookies with fondant icing. Decorate with black royal icing.

Fondant icing
Stir fondant in small heatproof bowl over small pot of simmering water until smooth. Add egg white; stir until smooth.

Royal icing
Sift powdered sugar through fine sieve. Beat egg white until foamy in small bowl with electric mixer; add powdered sugar, a tablespoon at a time. When icing reaches firm peaks, use a wooden spoon to beat in vanilla and coloring; cover surface tightly with plastic wrap.

Makes 28

frangipanis

1 stick plus 4 tablespoons
   butter, softened
1 teaspoon coconut extract
2 teaspoons finely grated
   lime zest
⅓ cup sugar
1½ cups all-purpose flour
¼ cup rice flour
⅓ cup unsweetened shredded
   coconut
¼ cup finely chopped
   candied pineapple
1½ tablespoons purple
   colored sprinkles

Fondant icing
10½ ounces white prepared
   fondant, chopped coarsely
1 egg white, beaten lightly
pink food coloring

1 Beat butter, coconut extract,
zest and sugar in small bowl
with electric mixer until smooth.
Stir in sifted flours, coconut and
pineapple in two batches.
2 Knead dough on floured
surface until smooth. Roll dough
between sheets of parchment
paper until ¼-inch thick.
Refrigerate 30 minutes.
3 Preheat oven to 325°F.
Grease rounded mini cake
pans (see page 116).
4 Using 3-inch flower cutter
(see page 123), cut 28 shapes
from dough. Place in cake pans
(see page 122).
5 Bake about 10 minutes. Cool
in pans.
6 Make fondant icing. Using
a metal spatula dipped in hot
water, spread pink icing quickly
over cookies. Sprinkle colored
sprinkles into centers of flowers.

Fondant icing
Stir fondant in small bowl over
small pot of simmering water
until smooth. Add egg white; stir
until smooth. Tint with coloring.

Makes 28

iced marshmallow butterflies

1 stick butter, softened
¾ cup sugar
1 egg
1½ cups all-purpose flour
¼ cup self-rising flour
½ cup unsweetened shredded
  coconut
⅓ cup unsweetened shredded
  coconut, extra

Topping

¼ cup strawberry jam, warmed,
  strained, cooled
160 mini pink marshmallows
160 mini white marshmallows

1 Beat butter, sugar and egg in small bowl with electric mixer until light and fluffy. Stir in sifted flours and coconut, in two batches.

2 Knead dough on floured surface until smooth. Roll dough between sheets of parchment paper until ¼-inch thick; refrigerate 30 minutes.

3 Preheat oven to 350°F. Grease baking sheets; line with parchment paper.

4 Using 1½-inch butterfly cutter (see page 123), cut 16 shapes from dough. Place 1¼ inches apart on baking sheets. Bake about 12 minutes.

5 Meanwhile, using scissors, quarter marshmallows. Press marshmallows cut-side down onto hot butterfly wings, trim marshmallows to the shape of the wings if necessary. Brush marshmallows with a little water; sprinkle with extra coconut. Bake about 1 minute or until marshmallows soften slightly.

6 Pipe jam down center of each butterfly. Cool on wire racks.

Makes 16

hazelnut chai teacups

You can make your own hazelnut meal by grinding skinned nuts in a nut mill or food processor until they reach the consistency of cornmeal.

1 stick butter, softened
1 teaspoon vanilla extract
¼ cup sugar
1 egg yolk
1 cup all-purpose flour
3 tablespoons self-rising flour
¼ cup cornstarch
1½ tablespoons chai tea
  (about 4 chai tea bags)
½ cup hazelnut meal
Fondant icing
10½ ounces white prepared
  fondant, chopped coarsely
1 egg white, beaten lightly
1 teaspoon lemon juice
yellow, blue and green
  food coloring
Royal icing
1½ cups pure powdered sugar
1 egg white

1 Preheat oven to 350°F. Grease baking sheets; line with parchment paper.
2 Beat butter, vanilla, sugar and egg yolk in small bowl with electric mixer until light and fluffy. Stir in sifted flours, tea and hazelnut meal.
3 Knead dough on floured surface until smooth; roll dough between sheets of parchment paper until ¼-inch thick.
4 Using 3-inch teacup cutter, cut out 14 shapes from dough. Place about 1¼ inches apart on baking sheets. Bake about 15 minutes. Cool on baking sheets.
5 Make fondant icing. Using a metal spatula dipped in hot water, spread icing quickly over cookies.
6 Make royal icing. Decorate cookies with royal icing.

Fondant icing
Stir fondant in small heatproof bowl over small pot of simmering water until smooth; stir in egg white and lemon juice. Divide among three bowls; tint yellow, blue and green with food coloring.

Royal icing
Sift powdered sugar through fine sieve. Beat egg white until foamy in small bowl with electric mixer; beat in powdered sugar a tablespoon at a time. Cover surface tightly with plastic wrap.

Makes 14

hazelnut shortbread trees

You can make your own hazelnut meal by grinding skinned nuts in a nut mill or food processor until they reach the consistency of cornmeal.

2 sticks butter, softened
2 teaspoons finely grated
   orange zest
½ cup powdered sugar
3 tablespoons rice flour
2 cups all-purpose flour
2 teaspoons allspice
¼ cup hazelnut meal
silver nonpareils
1½ tablespoons powdered
   sugar, extra

Brandy butter cream
5 tablespoons butter, softened
½ teaspoon finely grated
   orange zest
¾ cup powdered sugar
2 teaspoons brandy

1 Beat butter, orange zest and sifted powdered sugar in small bowl with electric mixer until light and fluffy. Transfer to large bowl. Stir in sifted flours and allspice, and hazelnut meal, in two batches.
2 Knead dough on floured surface until smooth. Roll dough between sheets of parchment paper until ¼-inch thick; refrigerate 30 minutes.
3 Preheat oven to 350°F. Grease baking sheets; line with parchment paper.
4 Using 1¼-inch, 2-inch and 3-inch star-shaped cutters (see page 123), cut 24 of each size star from dough. Place small stars, about ½ inches apart, on a baking sheet; place remaining stars, about ¾-inch apart, on baking sheets.
5 Bake small stars 10 minutes. Bake larger stars 15 minutes. Let stand 5 minutes; cool on wire racks.

6 Meanwhile, make brandy butter cream.
7 Sandwich two of each size cookies with butter cream. Assemble trees by joining three different size stars together with butter cream.
8 Decorate trees by joining nonpareils to stars with a tiny dot of butter cream. Dust trees with extra sifted powdered sugar.

Brandy butter cream
Beat butter, orange zest, sifted powdered sugar and brandy in small bowl with electric mixer until light and fluffy.

Makes 12

chocolate and cranberry checkerboards

1 stick plus 6 tablespoons
   butter, softened
¾ cup sugar
½ teaspoon vanilla extract
1 egg
2 cups all-purpose flour
1½ tablespoons cocoa powder
1 teaspoon finely grated
   orange zest
¼ cup finely chopped dried
   sweetened cranberries
1 egg white, beaten lightly

1 Beat butter, sugar, vanilla and egg in small bowl with electric mixer until light and fluffy. Stir in sifted flour in two batches.
2 Divide dough in half, knead sifted cocoa into one half; knead orange zest and dried sweetened cranberries into the other half. Using ruler, shape each batch of dough into 2- x 2- x 6-inch rectangular bars (see page 120). Wrap each in parchment paper; refrigerate 30 minutes.
3 Cut each bar lengthwise equally into three slices. Cut each slice lengthwise equally into three; you will have nine ½- x ½- x ½-inch slices of each dough (see page 120).
4 Brush each slice of dough with egg white, stack alternate flavors together in threes. Stick three stacks together to recreate the log; repeat with second log (see page 120). Refrigerate 30 minutes.

5 Preheat oven to 350°F. Grease baking sheets; line with parchment paper.
6 Using a sharp knife, cut each log into ½-inch slices (see page 120). Place, cut-side up, on baking sheets about 1¼ inches apart. Bake about 15 minutes. Let stand 5 minutes before lifting onto wire racks to cool.

Makes 30

baby shapes

You can make your own almond meal by grinding blanched almonds in a nut mill or food processor until they reach the consistency of cornmeal.

1 stick butter, softened
2 teaspoons finely grated
   orange zest
¼ cup sugar
1 egg yolk
1 cup all-purpose flour
3 tablespoons self-rising flour
¼ cup cornstarch
½ cup almond meal
1½ tablespoons finely chopped
   dried lavender or
   dried rose buds
Lemon icing
1 egg white
1½ cups powdered sugar
2 teaspoons all-purpose flour
2 teaspoons lemon juice,
   approximately
blue food coloring
Royal icing
1½ cups pure powdered sugar
1 egg white
blue food coloring

1 Beat butter, orange zest, sugar and egg yolk in small bowl with electric mixer until light and fluffy. Stir in sifted flours, almond meal and lavender or rose.
2 Knead dough on floured surface until smooth; roll between sheets of parchment paper until ¼-inch thick. Cover; refrigerate 30 minutes.
3 Preheat oven to 350°F. Grease baking sheets; line with parchment paper.
4 Using 5-inch bottle and 4½-inch carriage cutters (see page 123), cut 7 shapes of each from dough. Place 1¼ inches apart on baking sheets.
5 Bake about 12 minutes. Cool on baking sheets.
6 Make lemon icing; spread icing evenly over cookies.
7 Make royal icing. Decorate cookies with royal icing.

Lemon icing
Place egg white in small bowl, stir in half the sifted powdered sugar; stir in remaining sifted powdered sugar, flour and enough lemon juice to make a thick, spreadable icing. Divide icing among two bowls; tint one bowl with blue food coloring.

Royal icing
Sift powdered sugar through fine sieve. Beat egg white until foamy in small bowl with electric mixer; beat in powdered sugar a tablespoon at a time. Divide icing among two bowls; tint one bowl with blue food coloring. Cover surface of icing tightly with plastic wrap.

Makes 14

choc-mallow wheels

You will need 8 ounces of pink and white marshmallows for this recipe.

1 stick butter, softened
¾ cup firmly packed
   brown sugar
1 egg
1½ cups all-purpose flour
¼ cup self-rising flour
¼ cup cocoa powder
28 marshmallows
¼ cup raspberry jam
13 ounces dark chocolate chips
1½ tablespoons vegetable oil

1 Beat butter, sugar and egg in small bowl with electric mixer until combined. Stir in sifted flours and cocoa, in two batches.
2 Knead dough on floured surface until smooth. Roll between sheets of parchment paper until ⅛-inch thick. Cover; refrigerate 30 minutes.
3 Preheat oven to 350°F. Grease baking sheets; line with parchment paper.
4 Using 3-inch round fluted cutter, cut 28 rounds from dough. Place about 1¼ inches apart on sheets.
5 Bake about 12 minutes. Cool on wire racks.
6 Turn half the cookies bottom-side up; place on baking sheet. Use scissors to cut marshmallows in half horizontally. Press four marshmallow halves, cut-side down, onto cookie bases on baking sheet. Bake 2 minutes.

7 Melt chocolate in medium heatproof bowl over medium pot of simmering water. Remove from heat; stir in oil.
8 Spread jam over bottom of remaining cookies; press onto softened marshmallows. Let stand 20 minutes or until marshmallow is firm. Dip wheels into chocolate; smooth away excess chocolate using metal spatula. Place on parchment-paper-lined sheets to set.

Makes 14

1 cup all-purpose flour
½ cup self-rising flour
3 tablespoons instant vanilla
   pudding mix
⅔ cup powdered sugar
6 tablespoons cold butter,
   chopped
1 egg yolk
¼ cup passion fruit pulp
Butter icing
4 ounces unsalted butter,
   softened
1½ cups powdered sugar
3 tablespoons milk

passion fruit gems

1 Process dry ingredients and butter together until crumbly; add egg yolk and passion fruit pulp, pulse until ingredients come together.
2 Knead dough on floured surface until smooth. Roll between sheets of parchment paper until ¼-inch thick; refrigerate 30 minutes.
3 Preheat oven to 350°F. Grease baking sheets; line with parchment paper.
4 Using 1½-inch round flower-shaped cutter (see page 123), cut rounds from dough. Place about 1¼ inches apart on baking sheets.
5 Bake about 10 minutes. Cool on wire racks.
6 Make butter icing.
7 Spoon icing into piping bag fitted with a small fluted tube. Pipe stars onto cookies.

Butter icing
Beat butter in small bowl with electric mixer until as white as possible. Gradually beat in half the sifted powdered sugar, milk, then remaining powdered sugar.

Makes 70

slice and bake cookies

2 sticks butter, softened
1¼ cups powdered sugar
1 teaspoon vanilla extract
2 cups all-purpose flour
½ cup rice flour
⅓ cup cornstarch
3 tablespoons milk

1 Beat butter, sifted powdered sugar and vanilla in small bowl with electric mixer until light and fluffy. Transfer to large bowl; stir in sifted flours, in two batches, then milk.
2 Divide mixture in half. Knead each half on floured surface until smooth, then roll each half into 10-inch logs. Wrap each log in parchment paper; refrigerate about 1 hour or until firm.
3 Preheat oven to 325°F. Grease baking sheets; line with parchment paper.
4 Cut the logs into ½-inch slices; place about 1¼ inches apart on baking sheets. Bake about 20 minutes. Cool on wire racks.

Makes 48

Variations

Orange and poppy seed
Omit vanilla extract; beat 1½ tablespoons finely grated orange zest with butter and sugar. Add 3 tablespoons poppy seeds with sifted flours.

Lemon and cranberry
Omit vanilla extract; beat 1½ tablespoons finely grated lemon zest with butter and sugar. Stir in ¾ cup coarsely chopped dried sweetened cranberries with sifted flours.

Pecan and cinnamon
Add 1 teaspoon ground cinnamon to sifted flours, then stir in 1 cup coarsely chopped pecans. Sprinkle with cinnamon sugar before baking.

M&M's
Stir in 2½ ounces of mini M&M's with sifted flours.

coffee walnut creams

1⅔ cups all-purpose flour
1 stick cold butter, chopped
¼ cup sugar
½ teaspoon vanilla extract
1 egg, beaten lightly
18 walnut halves

Walnut butter cream
1 stick plus 5 tablespoons
  unsalted butter, softened
¾ cup powdered sugar
1½ tablespoons cocoa
1½ tablespoons instant
  coffee granules
1½ tablespoons hot water
1¼ cups walnuts, chopped finely

Coffee icing
1 cup powdered sugar
2 teaspoons instant
  coffee granules
1½ tablespoons hot water
1 teaspoon butter

1 Sift flour into medium bowl, rub in butter. Stir in sugar, vanilla and egg.
2 Knead dough on floured surface until smooth. Divide in half. Roll each half between sheets of parchment paper until ⅛-inch thick. Refrigerate 30 minutes.
3 Preheat oven to 350°F. Grease baking sheets; line with parchment paper.
4 Using 2-inch round cutter (see page 123), cut out 36 rounds. Place on baking sheets; bake about 12 minutes. Cool on wire racks.
5 Meanwhile, make walnut butter cream.
6 Sandwich cookies with butter cream; refrigerate 30 minutes.
7 Meanwhile, make coffee icing.
8 Spread cookies with icing and top with walnut halves.

Walnut butter cream
Beat butter and sifted powdered sugar in small bowl with electric mixer until light and fluffy. Beat in combined cocoa, coffee and the water. Stir in nuts.

Coffee icing
Sift powdered sugar into small heatproof bowl, stir in combined coffee and the water; add butter. Stir over small pot of simmering water until icing is spreadable.

Makes 18

You can make your own almond and hazelnut meals by grinding skinned nuts in a nut mill or food processor until they reach the consistency of cornmeal.

3 egg whites
¾ cup sugar
1¼ cups hazelnut meal
1½ cups almond meal
¼ cup all-purpose flour
3½ ounces dark chocolate, melted

1 Preheat oven to 325°F. Grease baking sheets; line with parchment paper.
2 Beat egg whites in small bowl with electric mixer until foamy. Gradually beat in sugar, one tablespoon at a time, until dissolved between additions. Transfer mixture to large bowl.
3 Fold in nut meals and sifted flour. Spoon mixture into large piping bag fitted with ½-inch plain tube. Pipe 3-inch sticks onto baking sheets.
4 Bake about 15 minutes. Cool on baking sheets 5 minutes; place on wire racks to cool.
5 Drizzle sticks with melted chocolate, place on parchment-paper-lined sheets to set.

Makes 34

nutty meringue sticks

pistachio shortbread mounds

You can make your own almond meal by grinding blanched almonds in a nut mill or food processor until they reach the consistency of cornmeal.

⅔ cup shelled pistachios, roasted
2 sticks butter, softened
1 cup powdered sugar
1½ cups all-purpose flour
3 tablespoons rice flour
3 tablespoons cornstarch
¾ cup almond meal
⅓ cup powdered sugar, extra

1 Preheat oven to 300°F. Grease baking sheets; line with parchment paper.
2 Coarsely chop half the nuts.
3 Beat butter and sifted powdered sugar in small bowl with electric mixer until light and fluffy; transfer to large bowl. Stir in sifted flours, almond meal and chopped nuts.
4 Shape rounded tablespoons of mixture into mounds; place about 1¼ inches apart on baking sheets. Press one whole nut on each mound; bake about 25 minutes. Let stand 5 minutes; place on wire racks to cool. Serve dusted with extra sifted powdered sugar.

Makes 35

chocolate lady's kisses

You can make your own hazelnut meal by grinding skinned nuts in a nut mill or food processor until they reach the consistency of cornmeal.

6 tablespoons butter, softened
½ teaspoon vanilla extract
¼ cup sugar
1 egg
½ cup hazelnut meal
¾ cup all-purpose flour
¼ cup cocoa powder
1½ tablespoons cocoa powder, extra

Choc-hazelnut cream

3½ ounces dark chocolate, melted
4 tablespoons butter
⅓ cup chocolate hazelnut spread

1 Beat butter, vanilla, sugar and egg in small bowl with electric mixer until combined. Stir in hazelnut meal, then sifted flour and cocoa.
2 Roll dough between sheets of parchment paper until ⅛-inch thick. Refrigerate 1 hour.
3 Make choc-hazelnut cream.
4 Preheat oven to 350°F. Grease baking sheets; line with parchment paper.
5 Using 1½-inch fluted cutter, cut 52 rounds from dough. Place on baking sheets.
6 Bake about 8 minutes. Let stand 5 minutes; place on wire racks to cool.
7 Spoon choc-hazelnut cream into piping bag fitted with large fluted tube. Pipe cream onto one cookie; top with another cookie. Repeat with remaining cookies and cream. Dust with extra sifted cocoa.

Choc-hazelnut cream
Beat cooled chocolate, butter and spread in small bowl with electric mixer until thick and glossy.

Makes 26

2 sticks butter, softened
1 teaspoon vanilla extract
½ cup firmly packed
   brown sugar
1 cup sugar
2 eggs
2¾ cups all-purpose flour
1 teaspoon baking soda
½ teaspoon ground nutmeg
1½ tablespoons sugar, extra
2 teaspoons ground cinnamon

1 Beat butter, vanilla and sugars in small bowl with electric mixer until light and fluffy. Add eggs, one at a time, beating until combined. Transfer to large bowl.
2 Stir in sifted flour, soda and nutmeg, in two batches. Cover; refrigerate 30 minutes.
3 Preheat oven to 350°F. Grease baking sheets; line with parchment paper.
4 Combine extra sugar and cinnamon in small shallow bowl. Roll heaping tablespoons of the dough into balls; roll balls in cinnamon sugar. Place balls 3 inches apart on baking sheets.
5 Bake about 12 minutes. Cool on baking sheets.

Makes 42

snickerdoodles

praline custard creams

You can make your own almond meal by grinding blanched almonds in a nut mill or food processor until they reach the consistency of cornmeal.

1 cup all-purpose flour
1¼ cups almond meal
6 tablespoons cold butter, chopped
1 egg yolk
1 teaspoon vanilla extract
3 tablespoons powdered sugar

Custard filling
⅓ cup sugar
¼ cup all-purpose flour
2 egg yolks
1 cup milk
1 stick butter, softened
1 teaspoon vanilla extract
½ cup powdered sugar

Almond praline
½ cup sliced almonds
½ cup sugar
3 tablespoons water

1 Make custard filling and almond praline.
2 Preheat oven to 325°F. Grease baking sheets; line with parchment paper.
3 Process flour, meal and butter until crumbly. Add egg yolk and vanilla; pulse until combined.
4 Knead dough on floured surface until smooth. Roll dough between sheets of parchment paper until ⅛-inch thick.
5 Using 1½-inch round cutter (see page 123), cut 72 rounds from dough. Place ¾-inch apart on baking sheets. Bake about 12 minutes. Cool on baking sheets.
6 Sandwich cookies with custard filling. Spread a little more custard filling around side of cookies. Roll cookies in praline then dust with sifted powdered sugar.

Custard filling
Combine sugar and flour in small pot; gradually stir in combined yolks and milk until smooth. Cook, stirring, until mixture boils and thickens. Simmer, stirring, over low heat, 1 minute; remove from heat. Cover surface of custard with plastic wrap; refrigerate until cold. Beat butter and vanilla until mixture is as white as possible. Beat in sifted powdered sugar. Beat in cooled custard, in four batches, until smooth.

Almond praline
Place nuts on baking-paper-lined baking sheet. Combine sugar and the water in small frying pan; stir over medium heat, without boiling, until sugar is dissolved. Bring to a boil; boil, uncovered, without stirring, until golden brown. Pour toffee over nuts; set at room temperature. Crush praline finely in food processor.

Makes 36

equipment

1. Piping bags
Available in various sizes from chefs' supply stores and cookware stores, these are usually made from a waterproof fabric. Bags can also be made from parchment or wax paper (see page 122); ideal for small amounts of icing.

2. Rounded mini-cake pan
Ideal for drying flowers, leaves, etc. (see page 122). Available from some supermarkets and cookware stores.

3. Plastic ruler
Used for measuring and straightening edges of dough in Chocolate and cranberry checkerboards, page 95.

4. Heart template
Used as a template in Mud cake sandwiches, page 56 (see also page 118).

5. Stamps
Available from craft stores in many shapes and sizes. Used in Girl-about-town latte squares, page 75 (see also page 118).

6. Plastic icing tubes
Can be bought from cake decorating suppliers, some craft stores, supermarkets and cookware stores.

7. Gingerbread people template
Available from craft stores. Used in Jigsaw gingerbread people, page 55 (see also page 119).

8. Rolling pin, spoon and brush
All available from cookware stores, some supermarkets and department stores.

9. Metal spatula
Available in various sizes from cookware stores, chefs' supply shops some supermarkets and department stores.

10. Popsicle sticks and skewers
Popsicle sticks can be bought from supermarkets and craft stores. Bamboo skewers can be bought from supermarkets and cookware stores.

11. Measuring spoons
Can be bought from supermarkets, chain stores and cookware stores.

12. Parchment paper
Used for making piping bags, lining baking sheets and cake pans. Available from supermarkets and cookware stores.

13. Colorings
Many types are available – supermarkets carry basic colors, and more unusual colors (pink, purple, black) are available at cake decorating suppliers and craft stores. All are concentrated; use a minute amount of any type of coloring first to determine its strength.

14. Strainer and edible glitter
Fine strainers are essential for sifting pure powdered sugar. Edible glitter is available from cake decorating suppliers.

15. Baking sheet and wire rack
Available from supermarkets, chain stores and cookware stores.

Shortbread buttons, page 79

To make neat buttons, place 2-inch round floured cookie cutter on parment-paper-lined baking sheet. Using a small teaspoon, press one rounded tablespoon of dough evenly inside the cutter. Remove cutter, wipe, dip in flour again, repeat with remaining dough.

To mark indented centers of buttons, use the lid of a plastic water bottle, dipped in flour. Mark holes in buttons using a bamboo skewer or knitting needle. Use a floured fork to gently mark pattern around edges of buttons.

Girl-about-town latte squares, page 75

To mark the squares clearly, use well-defined stamps such as high-heeled shoes, lips, handbags etc. Dip the stamps in flour, shake away any excess, then use to mark the squares of dough. Be sure to keep the stamps clean and re-flour between each use.

Mud cake sandwiches, page 56

Make a heart-shaped template from light cardboard, large enough to completely cover the top of the sandwiches. Place cocoa into a fine sieve, shake into the heart shape. Carefully remove template. Repeat with the remaining sandwiches.

cookie-making tips

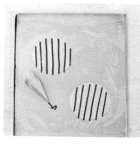

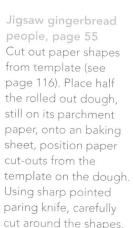

Jigsaw gingerbread people, page 55

Cut out paper shapes from template (see page 116). Place half the rolled out dough, still on its parchment paper, onto an baking sheet, position paper cut-outs from the template on the dough. Using sharp pointed paring knife, carefully cut around the shapes.

Carefully pull excess dough away from jigsaw shapes. Gently knead scraps of dough together on lightly floured surface. Re-roll dough between sheets of parchment paper to make more jigsaw shapes.

Ice-cream cones, page 40

Spread one rounded tablespoon of the plain mixture into the marked circles on the baking-paper-lined baking sheets. Fill a paper piping bag (see page 122) with chocolate mixture, snip end of bag, pipe chocolate stripes across the circles.

As soon as shapes feel slightly firm (not crisp) in the oven, remove the baking sheet from the oven. Working quickly, slide a knife or spatula blade under each shape to loosen; twist each circle into a cone shape. Place on a wire rack to cool completely.

Chocolate and cranberry checkerboards, page 95
Using the side of a plastic ruler, push and shape each piece of dough into the same size rectangular bar shape. Make sure all the sides of both bars are the same height, depth and width. Wrap each bar in baking paper; refrigerate 30 minutes.

Cut each bar lengthwise into three even slices, cut each slice into three lengths. You should have nine lengths from each bar.

Stack alternate flavors of lengths of dough, brushing each length of dough lightly but evenly with egg white as you stack. Start with three lengths, building up to nine lengths in each stack. Wrap each bar in parchment paper; refrigerate 30 minutes.

Use a sharp knife to cut bars into ½-inch-thick slices; place cut-side-up, about ¾ inch apart, onto parchment-paper-lined baking sheets.

  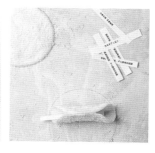 

Stained-glass lollipops, page 36

Using ½-inch round cutter, cut out 12 rounds from dough, place about 2 inches apart on parchment-paper-lined baking sheets. Starting from the centers of the cookies, use graduating sized round cutters to cut out lollipop shapes (see recipe). Remove excess dough from lollipops.

Brush dough evenly but lightly with lightly beaten egg white, then sprinkle with rainbow nonpareils if you like. Slide a popsicle stick under the circles of dough to the center of each lollipop. Proceed with recipe.

Coconut fortune cookies, page 23

Make sure you have all your messages ready. As soon as the cookies are baked, remove them from the oven; quickly slide a knife or spatula blade under each cookie to loosen them, then enclose a message in each.

Quickly position each warm cookie over the rim of a glass for 30 seconds to shape; place on wire racks to cool completely.

Frangipanis, page 87
Using 3-inch flower cutter (see page 123), cut out flower shapes from rolled-out dough. Place flowers into lightly greased rounded mini-cake pans (see page 116). Bake as directed in recipe. Cool flowers in pan.

The "Push" test
Most cookies baked on an baking sheet should feel a little soft after they've been removed from the oven, they become firm when they cool. If you're in doubt about the firmness, remove the cookies from the oven, then "push" one of the cookies on the sheet: if it slides, it's done, if it sticks, it needs more baking.

Paper piping bag
Cut a triangle (with all sides the same length) from wax or parchment paper. With the apex of the triangle pointing towards you, twist the triangle into a cone shape, by bringing all three points of the triangle together.

Fold the points over, secure with a staple or sticky tape. Fill the bag two-thirds full with icing etc, then fold the top of the bag over to enclose the filling. Snip a tiny piece from the end of the bag when ready for piping.

cookie cutters

We have used a wide variety of metal cutters, all shapes and sizes, throughout this book. They are available from cake decorator's shops, cookware stores, some department stores and craft stores. The measurements of the cutters used in the recipes were taken by measuring the longest/widest part of the cutter; for example, we measured a square cutter diagonally.

glossary

after-dinner mints mint squares coated in dark chocolate.

almond

extract synthetically produced; made with almond oil and alcohol or another agent.

meal also known as ground almonds; nuts are powdered to a coarse flour texture for use in baking or as a thickening agent. You can make your own by grinding blanched almonds in a nut mill or food processor until they reach the consistency of cornmeal.

sliced paper-thin almond slices.

apple juice concentrate made from apples; juice is extracted from the fruit, then pasteurized and evaporated under vacuum.

baking powder a rising agent consisting mainly of two parts cream of tartar to one part baking soda. The acid and alkaline combination, when moistened and heated, gives off carbon dioxide which aerates and lightens a mixture during baking.

baking soda a mild alkali used as a leavening agent in baking.

brandy short for brandywine, the translation of the Dutch "brandwijn," burnt wine. A general term for a liqueur distilled from wine grapes (usually white), it is used as the basis for many sweet-to-dry spirits made with fruits.

butter use salted or unsalted ("sweet") butter; 8 tablespoons is equal to 1 stick of butter.

buttermilk sold alongside fresh milk products in supermarkets and is commercially made, by a method similar to yogurt. Despite the implication of its name, it is low in fat and is a good substitute for dairy products such as cream or sour cream.

candied cherries boiled in heavy sugar syrup and then dried.

candied ginger fresh ginger root preserved in sugar syrup; crystallized ginger can be substituted if rinsed with warm water and dried before use.

candied pineapple pineapple cooked in heavy sugar syrup then dried.

caramels, hard confectionery item made from sugar, glucose, condensed milk, flour, oil and gelatin.

chai tea tea drink of India made with a mélange of spices ranging from pepper to cardamom to cinnamon.

chili, red Thai fresh, tiny, very hot and bright red in color. Serrano chilies are a good substitute.

chocolate

chips also known as chocolate morsels. Hold their shape in baking and are ideal for decorating.

dark made of cocoa liquor, cocoa butter and sugar.

milk most popular chocolate for eating; mild and very sweet, similar in make-up to dark with the difference being the addition of milk solids.

white contains no cocoa solids, deriving its sweet flavor from cocoa butter. Is very sensitive to heat.

chocolate hazelnut spread the most common brand is Nutella; made of cocoa powder, hazelnuts, sugar and milk.

cocoa powder also called just cocoa; unsweetened, dried, roasted then ground cocoa beans.

coconut

extract synthetically produced from flavoring, oil and alcohol.

shredded sold in sweetened and unsweetened varieties; concentrated, dried and shredded coconut.

coffee liqueur an alcoholic syrup distilled from wine or brandy and flavored with coffee. Use Tia Maria, Kahlua or any generic brand.

condensed milk a canned milk product consisting of milk with more than half the water content removed and sugar added to the milk that remains.

cornstarch available made from corn or wheat (wheaten cornstarch, gluten-free, gives a lighter texture in cakes); used as a thickening agent in cooking.

cream, heavy (minimum fat content 18%) homogenized and pasteurized, also known as whipping cream; commonly used in sauces, desserts and soups.

cream of tartar the acid ingredient in baking powder; added to confectionery mixtures to help prevent sugar crystallizing. Keeps frostings creamy and improves volume when beating egg whites.
currants, dried dried tiny, almost black raisins, so-named from the grape type native to Corinth, Greece. These are not the same as fresh currants, which are the fruit of a plant in the gooseberry family.
dark rum we prefer to use a lower proof rum for a more subtle flavor.
dried lavender available at specialist cooking stores.
dried rose buds available at specialist cooking stores.
eggs we use large chicken eggs having an average weight of 60g in our recipes unless stated otherwise. Some recipes may call for raw or barely cooked eggs; exercise caution if there is a salmonella problem in your community, particularly in food eaten by children and pregnant women.
food coloring vegetable-based substances available in liquid, paste or gel form.
flour
all-purpose unbleached wheat flour is the best for baking; the gluten content ensures a strong dough, which produces a light result.
rice very fine, almost powdery, gluten-free flour; made from

ground white rice. Used in baking, as a thickener, and in some Asian noodles and desserts.
self-rising all-purpose flour sifted with baking powder in the proportion of 1 cup flour to 2 teaspoons baking powder.
whole wheat milled with the wheat germ so is higher in fiber and more nutritious than white flours.
gelatin mix most commonly sold as Jell-O, a combination of sugar, gelatin, colors and flavors; when dissolved in water, the solution sets as firm gelatin.
hazelnut meal made by grounding the hazelnuts to a coarse flour texture for use in baking or as a thickening agent. You can make your own by grinding skinned nuts in a nut mill or food processor until they reach the consistency of cornmeal.
instant latte packets caffé latte-flavored milk powder; available from supermarkets.
jam also known as preserves; a thickened mixture of a fruit and sugar. Usually eaten on toast for breakfast, it's also used as a filling or icing for cookies and cakes.
lemongrass a tall, clumping, lemon-smelling and tasting, sharp-edged aromatic tropical grass; the white lower part of the stem is used, finely chopped, in much of the cooking of South East Asia. Can be found, fresh, dried, powdered and frozen,

in gourmet and organic grocery stores, as well as Asian food shops.
macadamias fairly large, slightly soft, buttery rich nut. Should always be stored in the fridge to prevent their high oil content turning them rancid.
malted milk powder a blend of milk powder and malted cereal extract.
maple syrup distilled from the sap of maple trees found only in North America. Maple-flavored syrup is not an adequate substitute for the real thing.
marshmallows made from sugar, glucose, gelatin and cornstarch; available in multiple colors.
marzipan a paste made from ground almonds, sugar and water; similar to almond paste but sweeter, more pliable and finer in texture. Easily colored and rolled into thin sheets to cover cakes, or sculpted into shapes for confectionery.
nonpareils miniscule ($\frac{1}{8}$ to $\frac{1}{4}$ inch) metallic-looking but edible confectionery balls used in cake decorating; available in silver, gold or various colors.
oat bran the hard and rather woody protective outer coating of oats which serves to protect the grain before it germinates.
parchment paper also known as silicon paper or non-stick baking paper; not to be confused with

index

waxed paper. Used to line pans before cooking and baking; also to make piping bags.

pistachio green, delicately flavored nuts inside hard off-white shells. Available salted or unsalted in their shells; you can also buy them shelled.

poppy seeds small, dried, bluish-grey seeds of the poppy plant, with a crunchy texture and a nutty flavor. Can be purchased whole or ground in most supermarkets.

prepared fondant also known as soft icing and ready-to-roll. Once found only in cake-decorating and baking supply stores, fondant is now carried in many supermarkets.

prunes commercially or sun-dried plums; store in the fridge.

rhubarb a plant with long, green-red stalks; become sweet and edible when cooked.

rolled barley sliced barley kernels rolled flat into flakes. Like rolled oats, rolled barley is usually served as porridge.

rolled oats flattened oat grain rolled into flakes and traditionally used for oatmeal. Instant oats are also available, but use traditional oats for baking.

sesame candy popular European candy of sesame seeds set in honey-toffee and pressed into thin bar-shapes. This flatter version can be harder to find than the smaller, brick-shaped version of the same treat; look for them in gourmet grocers and stores that carry international candies and sweets. They are also easily ordered online.

sugar

brown an extremely soft, fine granulated sugar retaining molasses for its characteristic color and flavor.

powdered also known as confectioners' sugar; pulverized granulated sugar crushed together with a small amount (about 3 percent) of cornstarch.

sugar-free lollipops small, individually wrapped fruit-flavored hard lollipops made with artificial sweetener.

vanilla extract obtained from vanilla beans infused in water.

vegetable oil extracted from plant sources.

wheat germ is the embryo of the wheat kernel, separated before milling for use as a vitamin-rich cereal or food supplement.

conversion chart

measures

The difference between one country's measuring cups and another's is, at most, within a 2 or 3 teaspoon variance, and will not affect your cooking results.

All cup and spoon measurements are level. The most accurate way of measuring dry ingredients is to weigh them. When measuring liquids, use a clear glass or plastic jug with graduated markings.

We use large eggs with an average weight of 2oz.

dry measures

IMPERIAL	METRIC
½oz	15g
1oz	30g
2oz	60g
3oz	90g
4oz (¼lb)	125g
5oz	155g
6oz	185g
7oz	220g
8oz (½lb)	250g
9oz	280g
10oz	315g
11oz	345g
12oz (¾lb)	375g
13oz	410g
14oz	440g
15oz	470g
16oz (1lb)	500g
24oz (1½lb)	750g
32oz (2lb)	1kg

liquid measures

IMPERIAL	METRIC
1 fluid oz	30ml
2 fluid oz	60ml
3 fluid oz	100ml
4 fluid oz	125ml
5 fluid oz (¼ pint/1 gill)	150ml
6 fluid oz	190ml
8 fluid oz	250ml
16 fluid oz (1 pint)	500ml
1 quart	1000ml (1 litre)

length measures

IMPERIAL	METRIC
⅛in	3mm
¼in	6mm
½in	1cm
¾in	2cm
1in	2.5cm
2in	5cm
2½in	6cm
3in	8cm
4in	10cm
5in	13cm
6in	15cm
7in	18cm
8in	20cm
9in	23cm
10in	25cm
11in	28cm
12in (1ft)	30cm

Oven temperatures

These oven temperatures are only a guide for conventional ovens. For fan-forced ovens, check the manufacturer's manual.

	°C (CELSIUS)	°F (FAHRENHEIT)
Very slow	120	250
Slow	150	275-300
Moderately slow	160	325
Moderate	180	350-375
Moderately hot	200	400
Hot	220	425-450
Very hot	240	475